The Assassination of Reinhard
the Top Nazi O

By Charles River Editors

Heydrich

About Charles River Editors

Charles River Editors provides superior editing and original writing services across the digital publishing industry, with the expertise to create digital content for publishers across a vast range of subject matter. In addition to providing original digital content for third party publishers, we also republish civilization's greatest literary works, bringing them to new generations of readers via ebooks.

Sign up here to receive updates about free books as we publish them, and visit Our Kindle Author Page to browse today's free promotions and our most recently published Kindle titles.

Introduction

Bundesarchiv, Bild 152-50-10
Foto: o.Ang. | 1934

The Assassination of Reinhard Heydrich (May 27, 1942)

"Since it is opportunity which makes not only the thief but also the assassin, such heroic gestures as driving in an open, unarmoured vehicle or walking about the streets unguarded are just damned stupidity, which serves the Fatherland not one whit. That a man as irreplaceable as Heydrich should expose himself to unnecessary danger, I can only condemn as stupid and idiotic." - Hitler

Cloak and dagger adventure, with daring commandos parachuted deep behind enemy lines to kill a sinister mastermind, belongs chiefly to the realm of thriller novels or films. However, World War II stretched over such vast territories and affected so many hundreds of millions of people that nearly every possible human interaction, from the vilest to the noblest, and from the most pedestrian to the exotically adventurous, achieved reality at some point during the conflict. The assassination of Reinhard Heydrich stands out as one of the war's most remarkable secret operations.

"The man with the iron heart," as Adolf Hitler dubbed him, made a fitting target for the dramatic events which unfolded in Prague on May 27th, 1942. According to testimony by the historian Michael Freund, "He is one of the greatest criminal figures of the Third Reich.

Nowhere in the histories of the Third Reich has [Heydrich] been awarded his rightful place. He is a man of outstanding significance, a criminal mind of Luciferic grandeur." (Dederichs, 2009, 17).

During the early stages of the war, the Reich Protector often walked the streets of Prague alone or with just one or two escorts, and he also favored an open-topped Mercedes 320-C convertible, which left him fully exposed to snipers, bomb throwers, and the like. Though he was ordered by the Fuhrer to install armored plates inside the seat backs to limit the effect of grenades hurled into the interior of his vehicle, these armor pieces remained idle in the castle garage on the date of Heydrich's assassination. By contrast, Heydrich found time to have expensive horsehair upholstery installed in the touring car, providing a springy, comfortable ride.

That would be all the good fortune a British-trained team of Czech assassins would need. Even though the assassination attempt was mostly botched (to the extent that the assassins initially assumed they had failed), shrapnel from an anti-tank grenade caused the top Nazi official severe injuries, killing him a little over a week later.

Even as Heydrich lay mortally wounded, Hitler and the Nazis planned severe reprisals, and the most notorious would come at Lidice, which the Germans tenuously (and incorrectly) linked to the plot. The Nazis ultimately razed the small village to the ground and killed every male over the age of 15 in town before sending the remainder off to concentration camps.

The Assassination of Reinhard Heydrich chronicles the plot to kill one of the top Nazi officials and the aftermath. Along with pictures of important people, places, and events, you will learn about the assassination of Heydrich like never before, in no time at all.

The Assassination of Reinhard Heydrich: The Czech Resistance's Killing of the Top Nazi Official during World War II

About Charles River Editors

Introduction

   Chapter 1: Heydrich's Background

   Chapter 2: Picking the Target

   Chapter 3: Operation Anthropoid

   Chapter 4: The Assassination

   Chapter 5: The Death of Heydrich

   Chapter 6: Vengeance

   Chapter 7: The Significance of Heydrich's Assassination

Online Resources

Bibliography

Chapter 1: Heydrich's Background

Heydrich in 1922

A tall, rather slender individual with a long face, prominent, narrowly aquiline nose, and small, slightly squinting eyes, Reinhard Heydrich wore his blond hair slicked back and possessed some of the accomplishments of a "gentleman." An intelligent administrator and skilled pilot, the man nicknamed "the Blond Beast" also played the violin with notable virtuosity due to the fact that his parents were an opera singer and a pianist. Despite those innocuous sounding positions, young Heydrich received frequent, brutal beatings from his mother, echoing the extraordinary levels of parental violence inflicted on many psychopathic killers during their formative years.

Standing alongside such bloodstained figures as Heinrich Himmler, Adolf Eichmann, and Hitler himself as the architect of a series of mass murders equaled in history only by those of the communists, Reinhard Heydrich emerges as a paradoxical individual from the surviving records. The Blond Beast showed great devotion to his wife, Lina von Osten, and his four children, daughters Silke and Marte and sons Heider and Klaus. Nevertheless, though he appears to have been unusually troubled by the horrors inflicted on Jews and foreigners during the Third Reich, Heydrich applied his iron will to force himself to continue whenever a pang of doubt occurred. In fact, Hitler groomed Heydrich as his potential successor, deeming him to be a suitable Fuhrer in the event of his own death or incapacity. Heinrich Himmler, head of the SS, viewed his nominal subordinate with a mix of proprietary paternalism, awe, and alarm, recognizing him as a useful protégé, admiring his grim handiwork, and fearing that the ambitious and intelligent man would supplant him by turns.

Heydrich standing alongside Hitler and Himmler in Vienna in 1938

As head of the Gestapo, Heydrich constructed the infamous "Nacht und Nebel, or "Night and Fog," program. This secret police operation was designed to abduct (and usually murder) enemies of the state with such care and secrecy that they simply vanished, with nobody witnessing their arrest or their transport to places of imprisonment, torture, or execution. "Nacht und Nebel" was designed to sow deep fear in the German populace, a program of "disappearing" enemies carried out in as eerie and ghostly a fashion as possible in order to give the Gestapo the aura of a haunting, invisible, omnipresent danger which could strike anywhere without warning.

Heydrich also involved himself heavily with the seizure and deportation of Jews, though he did not oversee their actual extermination, a matter handled by Adolf Eichmann. The Blond Beast did, however, help to gel Nazi policy during the early war years at the Wannsee Conference on January 20th, 1942, the infamous meeting where the Nazis decided the fate of Europe's Jews. The Nazis sensed distantly they might be defeated in the war, so they wished to complete at least some "work" prior to that moment. "Heydrich had stated at the Wannsee Conference: 'In the course of the implementation of the Final Solution, Europe is to be combed through from west to east. The evacuated Jews will be brought, group by group, to the so-called transit ghettos [...] to be transported from there further to the East.' The choice of the Lublin district as the center for the extermination actions could, therefore, serve as a cover for the claim that the Jews were being sent to the East. Their disappearance after their extermination in the death camps could be explained by saying that they had been sent further east." (Arad, 1987, 15).

A. Savin's picture of the building where the Wannsee Conference was held

Hitler was not present at the conference, which took place near one of the Wannsee lakes that form an important swimming attraction near Berlin, but the men present took their cue from the Fuhrer's statements, which included this diatribe: "I already stated [...] – and I refrain from overhasty prophecies – that this war will not come to an end as the Jews imagine, with the extermination of the European-aryan peoples, but [with] the annihilation of Jewry. For the first time the old Jewish law will now be applied: an eye for an eye, a tooth for a tooth ... And the hour will come when the most evil world-enemy of all time will have played out its role, at least for a thousand years." (Kershaw, 2008, 589).

A few months earlier, Hitler had appointed Heydrich "Reich Protector" of Czechoslovakia in late 1941, and once installed in his new post, the Gestapo chief set about conquering what was, in effect, his kingdom with a system he described as "whips and sugar," his own slant on the more familiar phrase "carrot and stick." Initially carrying out a number of political killings to show the Czechs he was not to be trifled with, Heydrich then treated his new subjects with a form of favor in order to win them over to the Nazi cause. In Poland, the Germans made themselves hated with their policy of random murder and grinding economic oppression, but Heydrich, by contrast, attempted to soothe the Czechs with high wages, good jobs, and various perquisites such as regular vacations in scenic areas for factory workers. At the same time, he left no doubt of the gruesome consequences of disobedience or rebellion. Heydrich was not exactly a kind master, but he attempted to create an unequal symbiosis which benefitted the Czechs as well – just not as much as it benefitted the Germans, of course.

As part of his program, Heydrich eschewed the trappings of security favored by most of his peers. Just as he had fearlessly confronted Russian fighters on the eastern front during the opening action of Operation Barbarossa, to the point of being shot down behind enemy lines and barely escaping with his life, now Heydrich defied potential death in a different fashion.

One of Heydrich's open air vehicles

Despite his steely rationality, Heydrich remained tormented by his own inner demons, as one bizarre incident in particular highlights: "One of his colleagues has described the haunting and profoundly revealing occasion when Heydrich came home at night to his brilliantly lit apartment and suddenly saw his reflection in a large wall mirror. In an attack of cold rage he 'whipped his pistol from his holster and fired two shots at this double', the ever and tormentingly present negation of himself." (Fest, 124).

Heydrich in Prague in 1941

Such was the man who was targeted for assassination by the British and the Czech government in exile as 1941 drew to a close. The British likely targeted him because of his association with Czechoslovakia, a nation whose fate made the English uncomfortable due to their partial culpability in its fall to Hitler's aggression. Neville Chamberlain had effectively signed away Czechoslovakia's independence in 1938 with the Munich Agreement, and for this reason the eastern European nation remained prominent in the thoughts of British statesmen who now viewed the appeasement policy as a mistake, if not outright treason.

Chapter 2: Picking the Target

The British Special Operations Executive, or SOE, and the Czechoslovakian government in exile under President Edvard Benes cooperated in creating the plan to kill Reinhard Heydrich. The operation received the somewhat bizarre codename "Operation Anthropoid" and originated with the Czech exiles. The British government placed increasing pressure on these displaced officials to come up with a plan bolstering Czech resistance to Nazi occupation. Accordingly, in September 1941, the Czechs picked Heydrich as an assassination target, and the SOE assisted preparations.

Benes

Wryly dubbed the "Office of Ungentlemanly Warfare," the SOE existed as a highly secretive wartime organization charged with clandestine operations against the Axis. In particular, the British government wanted the group to foment and assist resistance movements in occupied countries across Europe. Led in 1942 by Roundell Cecil Palmer, 3rd Earl of Selbourne, the SOE enjoyed little success during the early war years.

As if that poor track record wasn't enough cause for concern, the Czechs had divided support for the plan amongst themselves; in fact, powerful political disagreements amongst themselves characterized the Czechs during Germany's occupation. One faction, standing for democracy, wanted to see Czechoslovakia as an independent nation in the manner of France or Britain, and while the United States fully supported this faction, the British offered tepid, unenthusiastic assistance due in large part to the fact that they had signed away just such a state in the 1938 Munich Agreement and had difficulty admitting their error. The other Czechoslovakian faction espoused radical communist beliefs, called for the overthrow of the Western democracies assisting them, and wished to see Czechoslovakia become an effective province of the Soviet Union.

Portrait of Palmer

Despite these deep divisions, the Czech government in exile "gradually came to be identified with a distinctive concept of the strategy and tactics of that liberation. The London concept, for which Eduard Benes, the former president, was the main spokesman, was primarily national in content. Its aim was simple: the restoration of Czechoslovakia as an independent state, within its pre-1938 boundaries. Munich and its consequences were to be erased from history." (Skilling, 1960, 174).

However, the means necessary to attain this goal ran at loggerheads to long-established Czechoslovakian cultural norms. The Czech lands formed part of the Holy Roman Empire and then the Austrian empire for many centuries, making full independence from foreign domination a very recent phenomenon not only in fact but also in the Czech mindset. Originally a fierce and turbulent people, the Czechs successfully resisted the encroachments of the Empire for some time in the 1420s under the charismatic, violent, and unorthodox commander Jan Zizka, famous for his use of "war wagons" and artillery. The fanatical, reforming "Hussites" soon turned on themselves in bloody civil struggles, however, enabling crusaders from Western Europe to bloodily reestablish the hegemony of the Catholic church – and the secular power of the Holy Roman Empire – during the later 15th and early 16th centuries. Subjected to the torture, terror, and suppression characteristic of the Holy See's temporal extension of its influence, and a process of Germanization by the Imperial forces, the Czechs slowly lost their turbulent, warlike, freedom-loving character. They retained a certain independence of mind, but, ruled by forces far too powerful for effective direct resistance, became masters of manipulating their overlords without entering into outright conflict.

As a result, the idea of eschewing violence in favor of winning concessions through political maneuvering became deeply ingrained in the Czech mental and cultural milieu. Necessity remolded the descendants of Jan Zizka and the indomitable Hussites into a nation of self-aware collaborators who came to accept a measure of submission to foreign domination as a way of life, almost an inevitable natural order. "Until then, tyrannicide was entirely outside the context of the modern Czech political tradition. In the nineteenth century, the Czechs chose to settle their disputes with their Habsburg rulers through various forms of non-violent opposition. It was the institutionalized mass killing of both world wars, which to some seemed state-organized terrorism, that radically altered the situation." (Hauner, 2007, 86).

Accordingly, the Czechs themselves remained dubious as to the value of armed resistance against the Nazis. Only the Third Reich's brutality provided some catalyst to resistance beyond the Czech norms of manipulating and passively resisting their conquerors. Nevertheless, many Czechs remained opposed to killing Heydrich outright, with good reason, as the event proved. Deciding to kill Heydrich from the safety of well-appointed quarters in England was a far different matter than facing the consequences of the assassination on the ground in Czechoslovakia, and as it happened, the Czech resistance, after helping to set up the Heydrich assassination scheme, made an 11th hour attempt to persuade the government in exile to abandon it. On May 12th, 1942, just 15 days prior to the assassination, "several senior members of the Czech underground sent a radio message to London urging President Beneš to cancel the assassination, citing three major reasons: that thousands of hostages in German hands would be executed, that the Nazis would commence unprecedented massacres, and that the last remnants of the underground resistance would be wiped out." (Hauner, 2007, 88).

These fears proved to be eerily accurate, as every single one of them became a reality during the days following the attack on Reinhard Heydrich. By then, however, President Benes thought the plot was too far advanced to abandon, and the British remained sanguine that increased Czech resistance, or even a general uprising, would ensue once the Gestapo general died and demonstrated the human vulnerability of the Nazis.

Though the matter is disputed among historians, it is possible that Benes and his fellow Czech government exiles acted in response to a considerably more sinister motivation themselves. Though Heydrich contemptuously referred to his charges, in private, as "Czech garbage," and he privately claimed that only a minority of them presented suitable characteristics to make proper German citizens, his public actions paradoxically tended to make him more popular as time passed. Heydrich's initially bloody introductory period ended rather quickly, and while he continued to harry and deport Jews, the average Czech on the street began to profit from Heydrich's rule over Czechoslovakia. Whether Heydrich possessed the intelligence, lacking in so many other prominent Nazis, to realize that conquered peoples might be induced to support the Third Reich if the Germans offered benefits instead of oppression and murder, or whether Czechoslovakia simply had such high industrial value that the Nazis made an exception to their usual method of tormenting and impoverishing their foreign subjects, the "Blond Beast's" actions alarmed Benes in a different manner, according to some historians. One British historian provides a concise summary of President Eduard Benes' potential motivation for ordering Heydrich's assassination even in the teeth of heartfelt protests from his own nation's homegrown resistance movement: "The reason was not that Heydrich had inflicted a brutal regime of terror on the people of the Protectorate, but that he had been too soft on them and was winning their support. He had started his rule with all the harshness expected of him [...] After the stick came the carrot. Heydrich turned off the terror as quickly as he had started it, and proceeded to woo the Czech workers and peasants [...] with increased wages and rations [...] active opposition to German rule all but ceased [...] The only way to revive it was to provoke the Germans into a new wave of terror and repression." (Read, 2004, 750).

These represent serious charges which, if true, place Benes in the light of a ruthless man willing to deliberately trigger the murder of thousands of men, women, and children in his nation simply to retain his political influence among the survivors. If this assessment is accurate, then Benes emerges on the page of history as an unusual type of war criminal, deliberately provoking genocidal acts against his own nation and people in order to profit from their misery.

That said, in the absence of any documentary proof pointing precisely to Benes' thoughts on the subject, proving the government in exile's culpability remains difficult. Nevertheless, the suspicion, unlike many conspiracy theories, is not implausible, given the thorough, detailed warnings of Nazi retribution Benes received and the fact that he chose to ignore them entirely. These strong hints of malevolent intent cast doubts on the assassination of Reinhard Heydrich as an act of heroic tyrannicide and recast it more strongly as a cruelly selfish decision by exiled politicians determined to retain their own influence and luxurious lifestyle regardless of the human cost.

Chapter 3: Operation Anthropoid

The initial preparations for Operation Anthropoid commenced on October 2nd, 1941, seven months before they came to fruition, and the two men selected to carry out the actually killing were initially Josef Gabcik and Karel Svoboda. Svoboda did not remain on the roster long, however, due to an accident caused by a greatly accelerated timetable.

The SOE and Czech exiles conducted a supporting operation in early October entitled Operation Percentage, which involved dropping radios and their operators into Czechoslovakia to facilitate communications between the Czech resistance and Britain. However, the Gestapo located one of the main transmitters on the first night, seizing and torturing the operators to learn more details of what was underway. The Germans made use of what was, for their era, a high-tech solution; radio detecting vehicles prowled the streets of Czech cities, and once an illegal transmitter was detected, Gestapo agents closed in using small, belt-mounted Kapsch radio locators. This early man-portable tracking technology proved extremely effective, enabling a wave of arrests that alarmed both the British and the Czech government in exile.

Driven by fear that the Nazis would wipe out the resistance before their agents arrived to kill Heydrich, the SOE accelerated the timetable vastly: "The departure of the ANTHROPOID drop into the Protectorate was scheduled as early as October 7-10, 1941, on the basis of the first meeting of the intelligence department in London with the SOE. At that time a period of air operations over the occupied parts of Europe ended (a dark, moonless night was necessary for the long-distance flight)." (Burian, 2002, 35). While carrying out hasty parachute training, Gabcik and Svoboda met with near disaster when Svoboda struck his head on the ground during a botched jump and suffered severe injuries. Though they eventually healed, the injuries kept him out of Operation Anthropoid.

With Svoboda out of commission, the British substituted Jan Kubis, and training recommenced in Scotland. The two Czechs received thorough training in throwing grenades and bombs, firing various weapons (including Sten and Bren guns and Colt pistols), and parachuting. They also learned how to build and rig what are today referred to as IEDs (improvised explosive devices) but at the time fell under the umbrella term "booby traps." The third phase of their training featured orienteering in unfamiliar terrain, driving skills for a wide variety of military and civilian vehicles, and the use of Morse code. At the same time, British agents prepared extremely high quality false identification documents for the men, which even today remain scarcely distinguishable from actual "Czech Protectorate" documents issued by the Nazi government of

Reinhard Heydrich.

Gabcik

Kubis

While this training continued, the war entered a new period which eventually spelled the doom of the Third Reich. On December 7th, 1941, the Japanese attacked the American Pacific Fleet at Pearl Harbor, sinking ships and killing nearly 3,000 Americans. Hitler subsequently declared war on the United States, and though it was unclear at the time, it likely signaled the moment when victory for the Third Reich became impossible.

Even years before the D-Day landings and the brilliantly effective aggression of General George S. Patton, "the American Guderian" as the Nazis dubbed him, the entry of the United States into the conflict began to swing the weight of fortune against Germany. The Lend-Lease Program to the Soviet Union, later dismissed as contributing no more than 4% of the Soviet war effort by Stalin's postwar propagandists, actually provided between 30%-50% of Soviet materiel and food for the rest of the war, as revealed by Russian researchers examining the archives following the fall of the USSR. In some vital industries the figure climbed even higher; for example, 92% of the locomotive and train cars used by the Soviets to move troops and weaponry to the front originated in American factories (Weeks, 2004).

These events made it more imperative than ever that the Czech resistance begin operations to disrupt Nazi Germany's industrial heartland. At the same time, the SOE worried about funding cuts due to its lukewarm success at starting resistance movements and prompting full-scale uprisings elsewhere in Europe. They wanted a success it could brandish before the English government to justify its own existence.

Flight Lieutenant Ronald C. Hockey commanded the Halifax Mark II four-engine long-range aircraft which took off on the evening of December 28th, 1941 with Gabcik, Kubis, and a number of other Czech commandos on board. The aircraft left the ground at 10:00 p.m., flew over the English Channel to France, and turned east before reaching Darmstadt by 12:42 a.m. on December 29. Though harassed twice by German fighters, Lt. Hockey proved his skill by eluding the attackers on both occasions.

On the other hand, the insertion did not go as smoothly as the British had hoped. "Orientation for the crew was made very difficult because most of the reference points, such as railroad tracks, rivers, and even small towns, had disappeared under heavy snow cover. This fact contributed to a navigation mistake as the crew mistook Prague for Pilsen (from which they were shot at by an anti-aircraft battery at 2:12 a.m.). As a result, the ANTHROPOID group was air-dropped at 2:24 a.m. close to Nehvizdy, a village near Čelákovice, east of Prague, instead of east of Pilsen." (Burian, 2002, 44).

Lt. Hockey piloted his aircraft successfully back to Britain and, ultimately, survived the war. The men of the mission, in the meantime, found themselves in a snowy field with two containers of supplies, which included a Sten submachine gun, six anti-tank grenades, 32 pounds of plastic explosive, three pistols, and a variety of other armaments and tools. The men spent the first night hiding in the garden shed of a man named Antonín Sedláček, only to discover their proximity to Prague the following morning. They left for Pilsen immediately, since most of their contacts lived there, and soon found themselves ensconced in various safe houses. A doctor treated Gabcik, who injured himself during the nighttime, low-level parachute jump.

Making matters more difficult for themselves, the men left their equipment hidden outdoors in extremely rigorous conditions, a decision which nearly cost their mission its success. Weapons, like other sophisticated technological tools, must be kept dry and maintained to avoid the serious risk of failure. Gabcik and Kubis, however, concealed the grenades and Sten gun in sheds, exposed to bitterly cold temperatures and considerable moisture.

However, as fate would have it, the navigational error made by Lt. Hockey actually proved to be a boon for the assassins. The wary Germans detected the aircraft and combed the countryside for several days along its flight route, suspecting that agents entered the country via this means. However, the actual assassins had already moved to Pilsen, outside the area of search, meaning that the Gestapo and Wehrmacht men assigned to the search came up empty-handed. Other parachutists who landed around the same time did not fare so well; the Germans killed some, while others escaped only after desperate gun-battles in which they managed to kill their Nazi attackers in the snowy Czech countryside.

The men moved from safe house to safe house, spending as much time watching Heydrich's movements as possible. They noted his routes, his habits, and his typical schedule, and the Gestapo general's overall disdain for security also made itself evident during the months spent surreptitiously observing their quarry. Gabcik and Kubis grew convinced that two men could kill Heydrich, with a third acting as a spotter.

As the Czechs conducted reconnaissance, the local resistance leader, Bartos, an extremely sick man, anticipated the horrific consequences of the assassination and tried to dissuade the men from moving forward with Operation Anthropoid. The assassins initially kept their mission secret, but Bartos pieced the information together and confronted the men in April, just a month before the assassination took place. He begged them to reconsider in light of the massacres the Nazis would carry out to avenge Heydrich's death. Gabcik and Kubis met these demands with stony refusal and eventually stormed out in a rage: "The young men asserted that their mission was perfectly clear: they were to organize and carry out the killing. They were soldiers, so they could not find fault with the killing, or discuss its point or lack of point, its timeliness or its untimeliness. At the most, they might think it over; but they could do nothing against an order that they had been given." (MacDonald, 2007, 139).

Seeing that their pleas would not move the assassins, the resistance sent a message to London asking Benes to call off the mission, a request which the government in exile also spurned. Their suggestion that, in their own words, a "local Quisling" should be selected as a target also met with official refusal.

While this squabbling went on, the Gestapo managed to intercept and translate part of the Czech transmission, warning them that the Czechs planned some kind of commando operation in the near future. One unknown factor is whether the British SOE would have called off the operation had they known the resistance's objections and the probability of compromised communications. However, Benes and his lieutenants did not inform the English of the communication or the doubts it contained, and SOE itself did not learn of the dispute until after the end of the war.

Either way, the Gestapo formed a clear picture of rising Czech "terrorism," and Himmler himself grew alarmed enough to visit Prague on May 1st, slightly more than three weeks before Heydrich's assassination. The Gestapo noted large numbers of commandos and saboteurs, as well as the capture of explosives, booby-trapped telephones which exploded when a person lifted the receiver, and so on. Himmler asked Heydrich to improve the security situation in the light of these developments: "Heydrich approved all the general measures but categorically refused a personal escort on the grounds that it would damage German prestige in the Protectorate. A certain arrogant pride and his sporting outlook probably prompted his attitude. He really believed that no Czech would harm him. According to Heydrich's wife, he could not believe that the Czechs would risk national suicide by killing the Reichsprotektor." (MacDonald, 2007, 144).

The Anthropoid assassins received a final impetus to act from Heydrich's schedule; when Hitler called for the Gestapo general to return to Berlin on May 27th, 1942, the men knew this might be their last opportunity. Accordingly, they chose a killing ground suited to their purposes. Along the road from his castle to Prague, Heydrich drove down a hill to the Troja bridge in the Holešovice suburb, and at the bottom of the hill, the road went around an extreme hairpin turn, forcing all cars to slow to a crawl for several seconds to avoid skidding off the road. Moreover, a tram stop nearby provided the men with an excuse to loiter in the area without drawing unwanted attention, and no police stations or Gestapo barracks stood nearby. The plan was to kill Heydrich, either with a burst of fire from a Sten gun or with a hand grenade, then escape to nearby safe houses using bicycles.

The preparations and scouting had required so much time that the two men only prepared to carry out their orders on May 27th just a few hours before Heydrich left Prague by airplane for his meeting with Hitler in Germany, where he might possibly be given a reassignment to a different location. Operation Anthropoid would occur almost literally at the 11th hour.

Chapter 4: The Assassination

Reinhard Heydrich and the men planning to kill him both woke up to a beautiful morning on May 27, 1942. This was to be Heydrich's last day in Czechoslovakia for some time at least, and, apparently savoring a moment of pleasurable sentimentality, the Blond Beast abandoned his usual clockwork routine and driven punctuality. Instead, after rising at the Lower Castle in Panenské Břežany, he ate a leisurely breakfast, which only ended at around 9:00 in the morning.

A picture of the estate used by Heydrich in Panenské Březany

Once he finished his meal, Heydrich enjoyed some time with his family in the pleasant castle gardens, and the warm spring weather and fresh air made lingering on the spot a tempting proposition. While Lina, heavily pregnant with their fourth child, looked on fondly, the Man with the Iron Heart ran about the grounds, romping, laughing, and playing with his three small children. That scene offered stark contrast to the scenes of agony and death taking place in the extermination camps at that very moment, where Nazi guards harried Jewish parents and children by the thousands, striking them with whips and clubs or allowing German shepherds to tear at their naked bodies in order to drive them into the gas chambers where many would die standing, unable to fall in the densely packed mass of gasping, screaming, dying humanity.

Heydrich, his mind no doubt far removed from the scenes of horror for which he bore considerable responsibility, enjoyed an hour relaxing with his family before he finally climbed into his black Mercedes touring car. The car's open top allowed ample fresh air and sunlight, but it also exposed the occupants to bullets, grenades, and even such simple weapons as thrown rocks or roofing tiles. Only two men sat in the car: Heydrich, in the back seat, and his driver, Oberscharfuhrer (Staff Sergeant) Johannes Klein, in the driver's seat. Both were large men, with Heydrich standing 6 feet 3 inches tall and weighing 206 pounds, and Klein around 6' tall and likely outweighing his commander. While Heydrich remained lean and agile despite his size,

Klein's burliness made him clumsy and slow, though extremely strong. No escort accompanied the car as it rolled out of the castle gates past saluting sentries in the crisp uniform of the SS. Klein threw the car into gear and stepped on the gas pedal, speeding off in the direction of Prague along a route he had driven dozens if not hundreds of times before.

While Heydrich enjoyed a leisurely morning, the assassins found themselves in an agony of suspense while awaiting their target. Indeed, they almost abandoned their vigil for fear of being caught, and their worry about being noticed loitering around the Gestapo chief's route was no idle fear. Another assassin, from a very different source, had met a hideous fate just a few weeks before thanks to a chance discovery: "In March 1942, the Gestapo arrested a musician during a routine patrol at Warsaw's central railway station. Although his papers were in order and showed him to be a 'German musician' on his way to Prague, his over-sized, brand-new suitcase aroused suspicion. In a secret compartment, the Gestapo agents found a sniper's gun […] After days of brutal interrogations, the man cracked and confessed to being a Russian agent sent by Moscow to assassinate Heydrich." (Gerwarth, 2011, 276).

In contrast to their reprehensibly sloppy behavior during the five months leading up to this moment, Gabcik and Kubis acted methodically on the morning of the assassination attempt, and Josef Valcik accompanied them as a spotter. The men carried their weapons inside a pair of briefcases: "Inside, concealed under layers of grass, were the Sten gun, broken down into three pieces, and two fused bombs. The grass was intended to camouflage the weapons from a casual police check. Since the food shortages of 1941, many Czechs had started to breed rabbits and it was not unusual for citizens to collect food for their animals in the local parks." (MacDonald, 2007, 151).

Valcik

The men took a tram to the suburb where they had left their bicycles, retrieved them, and pedaled onward to Liben, where they took up their positions at the hairpin curve chosen as the ambush site. Valcik moved up the hill to a prearranged observation point, where he waited with his shaving mirror in his pocket to flash a signal to his comrades when he spotted the sleek black Mercedes convertible approaching.

Gabcik assembled his Sten gun underneath a light-colored raincoat he had brought for this purpose, then lurked as unobtrusively as possible near the tram stop as if he was waiting for one. Kubis, with his two grenades, stood on the opposite side of the street in the shade of a clump of trees, again trying to avoid drawing attention.

The three men positioned themselves for action by 9:00, but Heydrich, at that moment, was finishing his breakfast and walking out into the castle grounds to play with his sons. For the next 80 minutes, the three Czechs fidgeted, with their apprehension understandably growing as Heydrich failed to appear; after all, the longer they remained in one place and showing no interest in boarding the regular succession of trams or engaging in other normal business, the higher the chance that German police or Gestapo agents would spot them and move in for an arrest.

Finally, at 10:20 a.m. (some accounts say 10:32 or 10:35), Valcik spotted the black Mercedes 320-C convertible gliding down the street. A tram approached the hairpin turn from the opposite direction, but the assassins had already agreed that civilian casualties would be acceptable if necessary to carry out Heydrich's killing. Valcik pulled the shaving mirror from his pocket and flashed it in the sun in the direction of his comrades near the hairpin turn, and the two men saw the brilliant flash of sunlight off Valcik's mirror and prepared themselves for the moment of action.

As the Mercedes 320-C slowed to a walking pace to round the hairpin curve, Gabcik ran out onto the sidewalk, throwing aside the raincoat to level his Sten gun at the car and its two Nazi occupants. The Sten gun, a cheap 9mm submachine gun with a folding stock, featured a stamped metal build and a 32 round magazine. The British, whose long-standing gun control had thoroughly disarmed their populace and necessitated the importation of 5,000 donated firearms from the United States at the start of the war to provide the home guard with some kind of weaponry, had produced the Sten gun in vast numbers in an effort to arm their own forces and those of anti-Nazi insurgents throughout Europe.

The simple weapon, which fired pistol ammunition, seldom hit anything beyond 100 yards, but Gabcik stood just a few feet from his targets as he raised the Sten gun and squeezed the trigger. At this juncture, he learned another characteristic of the Sten: its tendency to stop working unless given constant maintenance to avoid a host of other problems and circumstances. Rather than a rattling burst of bullets shredding the two Nazis in front of him, the Czech heard only silence as he yanked frantically on the trigger. His Sten gun, brought so painstakingly to this point, was as useless as a toy.

At this moment, Heydrich and Klein each made a mistake that resulted in the Gestapo chief's death. Heydrich ordered his driver to stop, and Klein obeyed. Rather than accelerating out of the ambush, the aggressive Heydrich decided to capture or kill Gabcik, whom he incorrectly assumed was acting alone. Meanwhile, Kubis grabbed one of the anti-tank grenades out of his worn briefcase and sprinted out of the trees. The two Nazis, their attention focused on Gabcik, who still struggled futilely with his Sten gun a few feet away, would fail to notice the second attacker until it was too late.

Kubis acted decisively but clumsily. "He misjudged his throw. Instead of landing inside the Mercedes, it exploded against the rear wheel, throwing shrapnel back into Kubiš' face and shattering the windows of the tram which had stopped on the opposite side of the road. There were screams as the passengers were hit by shards of flying glass and metal. The car lurched violently and came to rest in the gutter, pouring smoke. Two SS jackets which had been folded on the back seat were whirled upwards by the blast and draped themselves over the trolley wire." (MacDonald, 2007, 153).

Pictures of the damaged car and tram

Despite the poor toss, Heydrich had suffered severe injuries in the blast, the worst being a large piece of shrapnel which ripped through his back and deep into his spleen. However, the Gestapo chief was so full of adrenaline that he didn't feel his injuries, and thinking he was unharmed, he jumped out of the car and staggered towards Gabcik, trying to get a clear shot with his 7.65mm pistol. Gabcik stood for several moments, staring stupefied at the tall, blond man in the black uniform stumbling towards him through the smoke and dust. Then, despite the shock of the explosion, the Czech made a stumbling run uphill. As he fled, the crack of pistol shots sounded behind him, and bullets whined past him. Desperately, he jumped behind a telephone pole and fired back at his black-garbed pursuer. Heydrich moved behind the damaged tram and returned fire, hoping to cripple or kill Gabcik.

Gabcik began to despair, knowing that SS men would arrive on the scene very soon. However, as the gunfight continued, Heydrich suddenly dropped to the ground; the pain from his wound suddenly struck him, and he writhed in agony for several moments. Gabcik, terrified, did not return to finish his target off but fled uphill, diving through the open door of a butcher shop up the road.

As that was going on, Klein pursued Kubis. The huge Nazi was slow-moving, but Kubis was scarcely faster. His forehead torn open by shrapnel from his own poorly-thrown grenade, the Czech assassin found it hard to flee with blood dripping into his eyes. He staggered to the place where the bicycles stood and leaped onto one, pedaling away frantically and leaving the raging Klein far behind him in a matter of moments.

Klein returned to find Heydrich lying on the ground next to the tram. His first instinct was to help his wounded chief, but Heydrich, pointing in the direction of Gabcik's flight, managed to snap at him, "Get that bastard!" Heydrich then reeled back to his feet and stumbled back to the car, where he fell across the hood and lay for some time. Klein thundered up the hill, but his pistol was jammed, so he would need to grapple with Gabcik should he spot him. As he reached the top, a man in a butcher's apron ran out of a shop and pointed back inside, shouting that a man with a pistol was hiding inside. Klein charged in the front door and slammed into Gabcik, who was running out at the same moment. The butcher, Bauer, was a Nazi sympathizer, and Gabcik had just discovered that the butcher shop had no back door or windows.

Finding himself in the iron grip of the enormous, enraged Klein, Gabcik fired a shot from his pistol that punched through both of the huge German's legs. Klein fell to the ground, roaring in pain and anger, while Gabcik leaped over him and ran wildly away. Klein managed to drag himself to his feet and pursue despite his wounds, but Gabcik managed to elude him in the alleys and take cover more successfully.

In the meantime, the final drama of Heydrich's life unfolded at the bottom of the hill. A young woman with blonde hair and a Czech policeman frantically flagged down passing vehicles to drive the Gestapo general to a hospital. The two Czechs stopped a bakery van first, but the driver, frightened, refused to help and eventually drove off. The man at the wheel of a second van, loaded with floor wax, showed more boldness. The bystanders placed Heydrich on his stomach in an effort to keep dirt out of his back wound, and the van drove off through the streets in the direction of the hospital.

Chapter 5: The Death of Heydrich

Despite the severity of his injuries, the mortally wounded Heydrich did not die shortly after the grenade seriously injured him. In fact, he lived for more than a week, dying eight days later on June 3rd at precisely the moment his relieved doctors believed he was about to make a full recovery. Two main theories as to his cause of death posit that he was killed by an infection, exacerbated by horsehair from the car's seat cushions carried into his wounds by the grenade fragments, or that botulism deliberately placed in the grenade by British SOE agents effected his demise. However, a third possibility – a lethal embolism caused by a postoperative blood clot – appears the most likely from evidence.

In the wake of the attack, the wounded Gestapo general was taken to the large, 1,400 bed Bulovka Hospital in the only vehicle immediately available, a delivery van carrying tins of wax. By the time he reached the hospital, Heydrich needed urgent medical care but initially refused it, perhaps distrusting Czech doctors and surgeons, but once several German doctors quickly put in an appearance, Heydrich consented to surgery.

A large hole in Heydrich's lower back, bleeding heavily and filled with metal fragments and debris, was only one of several bad injuries he had sustained. The doctors discovered, via x-ray, that the grenade had also collapsed the Nazi leader's left lung and punctured his spleen. Fortunately for him, his kidneys proved intact and the fragments missed his spine by a wide margin, raising his chances of survival considerably.

Despite Heydrich's openly expressed misgivings, the doctors took their medical calling seriously and provided the best care they could to their patient. Regardless of their personal feelings about the Blond Beast, both Czech and German doctors acted with professionalism and treated Heydrich with the same care and attention to correct medical procedure as they would have for any other patient. Fear of retribution doubtlessly provided some motivation, but the men involved clearly also adhered scrupulously to the neutrality demanded by their merciful profession, unlike notorious medicos such as Dr. Josef Mengele or Dr. Helmut Poppendick.

The operation began within an hour of Heydrich's arrival at Bulovka Hospital, and after the doctors inflated the Blond Beast's left lung and administered anesthesia, they gave Heydrich the first of two blood transfusions, along with antitoxins intended to prevent lethal gangrene. Dr. Walter Dick began the procedure by cleaning Heydrich's chest wound and removing the shattered tip of one of his ribs, then sutured that and several other wounds after thorough cleaning.

The next stage, involving the removal of Heydrich's badly damaged spleen, fell to Dr. Josef Hohlbaum, but the surgeon proved unable to continue due to an attack of nerves. "Dr. Hohlbaum, now wearing his glasses, made an incision from sternum to mid-abdomen. As he was reaching the umbilicus, Dr. Honek noticed that he was perspiring profusely. Dr. Dick reacted at once, and in his usual quiet and courteous manner whispered, 'Professor Hohlbaum, you are not well, allow me to take over.'" (Defalque, 2009, 4).

Dr. Dick continued the procedure and discovered that the explosion had nearly destroyed Heydrich's spleen. A three-inch-square piece of grenade casing had lodged in the ruptured organ, carrying huge clumps of horsehair into the German's body along with it. The doctor removed the spleen and finished the suturing job, after which the doctors administered a second transfusion. Heydrich's vital signs remained strong and stable throughout, and the procedure took almost exactly an hour. The doctors moved the Gestapo general to a private hospital room at 2:00 p.m.

All the while, the SS established a strong guard in the hospital wing where Heydrich lay, ejecting the other patients and allowing only specific doctors and nurses whom they trusted to enter that portion of the building. Lina Heydrich soon arrived to see her husband, and Heydrich recovered quickly from the anesthesia and proved able to converse with her within an hour of the surgery's end.

Himmler sent three of his best SS surgeons - Dr. Karl Gebhardt, Dr. Stumpfegger, and Dr. Ferdinand Sauerbruch - to care for his wounded protégé. The trio arrived by airplane that same evening and took over within two days from Dr. Dick and his associates. The SS doctors declined to administer antibiotics, distrusting them because they espoused an early anti-vaccination stance due to their belief that vaccines represented a Jewish plot against Aryan health. In any case, the Germans did not yet have access to penicillin, relying instead on inferior sulfonamides.

Gebhardt

Sauerbruch

Heydrich developed an infection and fever, but on June 3rd, he appeared to rally. His fever abated, and he grew far stronger and more active. Around noon that day, he felt strong enough to sit upright in bed and eat a hearty meal, but in the middle of it, he suddenly fell over unconscious. Comatose, he died early in the morning of June 4th despite the doctors' attempts to save him. The medical staff meticulously noted his death in the hospital death register, and the doctors completed an autopsy which confirmed a lung infection and fluid in and around the lungs. However, it is now known that the amount of fluid found and measured by the doctors is considerably below the threshold usually needed to cause death, particularly in a large, healthy 38-year old man. Suggestively, the autopsy found large fat particles in Heydrich's heart, one of the symptoms of a major cardiac embolism. This, in turn, would have led to a cerebral embolism producing exactly the observed symptoms: a sudden collapse, coma, and, without modern treatment, death. The attack occurred when Heydrich sat up after remaining largely prone for a week, and a change of position that could easily dislodge a blood clot accumulated during a long period of inactivity.

British microbiologist Paul Fildes later claimed Heydrich's death as a personal trophy, asserting that he placed quantities of botulism toxin into the grenades and that this caused Heydrich's death. The facts indicate this sensational scenario lacks basis, save in Fildes' well-known self-aggrandizing imagination. Botulism toxin produces paralysis, and at no point during his illness did Heydrich show any signs of paralysis in any form. Most other botulism symptoms also failed to appear, and Kubis and Maria Sochmanova suffered wounds from the same grenade and never fell sick.

Furthermore, even if the British added botulism to the grenades, the attempt would have failed. The Czechs stored the grenades outdoors for five months, much of that time in wintry weather, which likely would have destroyed the toxin in any case. Botulism toxin breaks down rapidly in temperature extremes, and the bitter cold of early 1942 would've likely done it.

Lastly, since the Germans recovered an unexploded grenade from the set Kubis carried, proof exists that it was an ordinary anti-tank grenade with part of its shell removed and replaced by regular adhesive tape. This made the grenade easier to carry due to lessened weight but decisively compromised the sealed internal environment the explosive device would have needed to have even a slight chance of keeping the toxin stable enough to reach its target in a useful condition.

Reinhard Heydrich received a state funeral from the Third Reich in a gigantic Berlin ceremony. After lying in state for two days in the courtyard of Prague Castle, the Gestapo general's remains journeyed by aircraft to the Reich's capital, where he was laid to rest amid solemn speeches by prominent Nazis (including Adolf Hitler himself) to the sound of the funeral march from the "Twilight of the Gods" by Richard Wagner.

A picture of Heydrich's funeral

Brooding, menacing, filled with a bleak and sweeping grandeur, the strains of Wagner's magnificent composition served to mark the obsequies of more than just one Nazi official. They became, effectively, the dirge for thousands of other luckless human beings as well. The Third Reich exacted a hecatomb of revenge on the Czech people for the decision of their leader in faraway London: "Hitler exclaimed bitterly that Heydrich's death was like a 'lost battle', and the regime reacted with the savagery displayed by primitive peoples at the graves of their tribal chiefs and demigods." (Fest, ,133).

Thousands would bleed and die for the Reich Protector as the Nazis sent him on his final journey. Himmler, speaking at the Blond Beast's funeral, evoked the dreadful code of racial supremacy and genocide by which the intelligent, gloomy, psychopathic Gestapo general had lived, and which served as the glue holding together the remarkably varied band of misfits Hitler assembled to stand at the helm of the Thousand Year Reich. Himmler declared that in life, Heydrich was "feared by the sub-humans, hated and slandered by Jews and other criminals [...] From the deepest reaches of his heart and his blood, he felt, understood and realized the worldview of Adolf Hitler. He seized all the tasks he was charged with from his fundamental comprehension of a genuine racial worldview and from the knowledge that the purity, security and defence of our blood is the supreme law." (Gerwarth, 2011, 279).

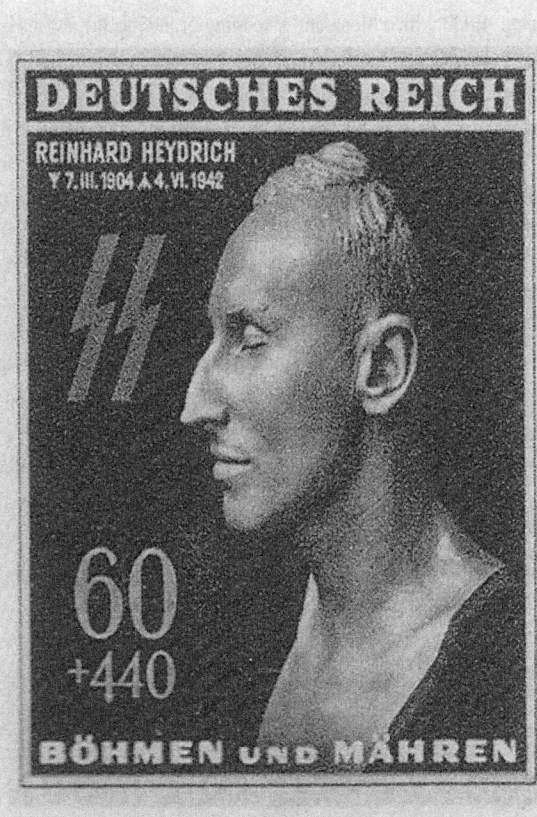

A 1943 postage stamp depicting Heydrich's death mask

Chapter 6: Vengeance

Predictably, the Germans responded furiously to the brazen attack on a high Nazi official, which included launching an immediate manhunt for the perpetrators. While Reinhard Heydrich's troubles were, in a sense, over, those of Czechoslovakia were only just beginning.

Helmuth von Pannwitz, the chief of the Prague Gestapo's anti-sabotage branch, raised the alarm after he investigated a vague Czech police report of assassins wounding a German officer and found Heydrich being prepped for surgery at the Bulovka hospital. The other Nazis initially believed Pannwitz's report to be a practical joke, but his desperation eventually convinced them and a large detachment of heavily armed SS moved to the hospital to defend the "Reich

Protector."

Pannwitz

Pannwitz and the local Wehrmacht commander, Karl Hermann Frank, began an investigation which soon blossomed into a manhunt. Pannwitz, interrogated in the Lubyanka by the Soviet secret police (NKVD) after the war, would be sent to a Soviet gulag for 10 years before eventually being sent back to Germany in 1956 and working as a salesman until his death in 1975. In June 1942, however, he investigated the attack scene thoroughly, and he "was convinced straightaway that the assassins were parachutists. The unused bomb contained British plastic explosive, British fuses and British detonators: 'Because the sub-machine-gun was also British, there was no doubt as to where the assassination had been organized." (MacDonald, 2007, 156).

As news of the attack spread, ordinary Germans in the region grew enraged and began attacking Czechs, throwing bricks or firebombs into Czech stores and trying to kill Czechs they had lived alongside all their lives. The Gestapo and ordinary police protected the Czechs from this violence, which would lead to social disorder, but ultimately, the cruelty to be visited on the Czechoslovakian population would be officially organized, not a matter of vigilantism.

Hitler himself responded with a characteristic lack of restraint when he learned of Heydrich's wounding at 12:45 p.m. on May 27: "Infuriated, the Fuhrer ordered the arrest and execution of 10,000 Czech hostages. [...] German police collected all available evidence and concluded the attack must have been organized and prepared in England. Frank telephoned Hitler to confirm the British involvement and asked him to revoke the execution order, arguing that such unprecedented reprisals would be catastrophic for Czech morale." (Hauner, 2007, 85).

Though Hitler agreed to stop the immediate execution of 10,000 Czechs, he remained adamant that blood must be spilled in response to the attack. The Third Reich offered a reward of 10 million Czech koruna ("crowns") for information leading to the hiding place of the assassins, and at the same time, the highest members of the Nazi hierarchy discussed what response to the assassination attempt would be most appropriate. Propaganda minister Joseph Goebbels voiced fear that assassinations would multiply if they did not offer an overwhelming response: "It is imperative that we get hold of the assassins. Then a tribunal should be held to deal with them and their accomplices. The background of the attack is not yet clear. But it is revealing that London reported on the attack very early on. We must be clear that such an attack could set a precedent if we do not counter it with the most brutal of means." (Gerwarth, 2011, 11).

Goebbels

The manhunt launched by Pannwitz, Frank, and the Orpo police general Kurt Daluege soon reached unprecedented proportions. In an effort to get the assassins should they try to leave the city rather than remaining in hiding, the Germans suspended all railway and most tram services for the duration of the emergency. With martial law in place, Pannwitz and Frank enforced a 9:00 p.m. – 6:00 a.m. curfew, and the Nazis decreed that all Czechs, on pain of death, must obtain new identity papers before May 29th, with their families also subject to execution if they failed to comply.

Daluege

With these preliminary steps taken, the German commanders began their work in earnest. They mobilized 12,000 men, including men from the Gestapo, Wehrmacht, SS, Orpo, and the Czech police force, and began a massive sweep of Prague. The Germans searched over 36,000 buildings, yet, amazingly, discovered no clue as to the assassins' location, even though Gabcik, Kubis, and six other resistance personnel occupied a central position in the city of Prague the whole time. The men moved from one safe house to another for several days until they found their way to the Karel Boromejsky church at the city's heart. There, they hid themselves in the dim crypt beneath the white-walled stone building, already effectively buried and spending their days among the dead of centuries past. News reached them of Heydrich's death and the hideous vengeance extracted by the Germans, and while the first news cheered them, all of the men – and the two assassins, Gabcik and Kubis, in particular – felt a deep sense of guilt for the terror unleashed by the Nazis in response to their actions.

Gabcik and Kubis eventually concocted a scheme which they hoped would put a stop to the Germans' program of revenge killing. The two men initially thought to go to a public park and shoot themselves there while wearing placards declaring their sole guilt in Heydrich's assassination. They then altered their plan to instead go to the office of Emanuel Moravec, a prominent Nazi collaborator, confess to the assassination of Heydrich, then kill Moravec also before taking cyanide pills. However, the other resistance men sharing their refuge talked them out of these steps, arguing – probably correctly – that the Nazis would continue their massacres regardless of the gesture.

Eventually, Pannwitz acted as what might be called the voice of reason among the Nazis. He believed that the far-flung terror tended to silence those who knew something of the assassins out of fear that they and their families would be executed for not speaking up sooner. "'Our special squads ... confirmed again and again the opinion of the criminologists that fear and anxiety kept back even those who might normally have been prepared to give some information no matter from what motive.' [...] The proposition was put to Frank, who issued a proclamation on 13 June promising that anyone who by 18 June denounced the assassins or provided the police with information leading to their arrest would not be harmed." (MacDonald, 2007, 169).

This measure prompted the breakthrough the Germans hoped for when an anonymous letter arrived at Gestapo headquarters, among 200 other letters, naming Gabcik and Kubis as the two men who killed Heydrich and pleading with the Nazis to stop killing people who had nothing to do with the assassination. A day later, the letter's writer, a Sergeant Curda, walked into Gestapo headquarters and gave himself up. Stammering in acute terror, he gave the Germans the names of those involved in the plot. A parachutist himself and a brave soldier earlier in the war, Curda appears to have simply grown sick of the slaughter and believed that Benes' scheme to kill Heydrich was the act of a man detached from the real, actual horrors his decisions inflicted on the people of Czechoslovakia.

Curda did not know where the assassins were hiding, but he was able to betray the location of several safe houses. The Gestapo arrived at the apartment of the Moravec family early in the morning on June 17th. Battering at the door with their rifle butts, the Nazis shouted for the parachutists. The secret police bundled Mr. and Mrs. Moravec and their 17 year old son Vlastimil (nicknamed "Ata") into the hallway while they violently ransacked the apartment. Astonishingly, the Gestapo permitted Mrs. Moravec to visit the toilet, where she swallowed cyanide and quickly perished. Her husband and son did not gain such a merciful release.

The Gestapo quickly determined that Mr. Moravec possessed no knowledge of the resistance, and that it was his wife and son who had helped the assassins. Since Mrs. Moravec was already dead, the Germans took Vlastimil to the basement of the Petek Palace and subjected him to continuous torture for nearly 16 hours. Screaming under the whips, pliers, and electrodes of the Gestapo, Vlastimil showed almost superhuman determination, refusing to tell his tormentors anything.

Finally, the Germans, probably fearing he would die under torture rather than divulge the information they needed, tried a different tack; the Gestapo brought large quantities of brandy and forced Vlastimil to consume it. When he was thoroughly drunk but still conscious, the final, bizarre touch intended to break his resistance was brought in. Struggling to focus through the waves of agony washing through his body and the alcohol clouding his mind, Vlastimil squinted at the object the German in front of him held out. Suddenly, the hideous, surreal sight came into focus: the Gestapo interrogator was holding a fish tank half full of water, and bobbing obscenely on the surface was the severed head of Vlastimil's mother. As the stunned teenager stared at this gory object, deliberately presented in as weird and surreal a manner as possible, he heard the voice of a German warning him that his father would also be decapitated unless he told the Gestapo everything he knew about the parachutists.

With that, Vlastimil's spirit broke and he began to talk. He revealed that his mother had indeed aided the parachutists. Though he did not know if they were currently there, he had also heard her mention that the crypt of the Karel Boromejsky church was the place he should flee if the Gestapo ever discovered their secret.

Pannwitz figured immediately that this was the hiding place of the fugitives. As quietly as possible, 700 elite Waffen SS men moved into position around the church, and the Germans sealed the manhole covers for many blocks around in case the Czechs could somehow reach the sewer system. Then, as day started breaking, Pannwitz led a number of SS men into the church itself.

The Germans soon discovered three of the parachutists had moved to the prayer loft, weary of the depressing surroundings of the crypt. The first German attempt to enter the loft ended when the Czechs rolled live grenades down the steps from above, sending the SS men scurrying for cover. Eventually, the SS men fought their way up into the loft.

There, in the gloom amid the ancient church pillars, a ferocious gun battle erupted, during which the three Czechs held off superior German numbers for over two hours. Finally, two of the men died outright. The Germans found the third still alive but unconscious; this was the grenade-thrower, Kubis. The Nazis made every effort to save the wounded man's life so that he could be interrogated later and perhaps used for anti-British propaganda purposes, but Kubis bled to death within 20 minutes without regaining consciousness.

Picture of damage done inside the church during the fighting

The Germans bottled up the other four men in the crypt but found themselves faced with the problem of how to remove them from that place alive. The Germans initially tried to persuade them to surrender by enlisting the services of the church's preacher, Petrek, who was attempting to save his own life, and their two prisoners, Moravec and Curda. "Loudspeaker announcements were soon reverberating through the morning air, promising that the parachutists would be treated as prisoners of war if they surrendered peacefully. Petrek was sent up to the grille to talk to them but they answered defiantly, shouting that they were Czechs and would never surrender. Karel Curda and Ata Moravec were brought to the church, handcuffed to Gestapo men. Moravec refused to help the Germans but Curda approached the vent and called: 'Surrender, boys, it will be all right.' He was greeted with a volley of shots which sent everyone ducking for cover." (MacDonald, 2007, 174).

The Nazis next used a fire engine to pump vast quantities of water into the crypt while throwing smoke bombs and tear gas grenades in, hoping to flush the men out alive. The resourceful Czechs used a ladder to reach the opening where the fire hoses entered and reached out to puncture them with their bayonets.

The Waffen SS next tried a direct assault but, in the waist-deep water in the crypt, found themselves under a galling fire from niches in the crypt walls. They fled back up the narrow stairs, carrying their wounded with them.

As Frank and his infuriated SS prepared to blow part of the church up, the sound of four gunshots echoed up from the dripping stairs. The last four Czechs, running low on ammunition, had killed themselves to avoid the long, torturous death the Germans would have inflicted on them had they been captured alive. 14 Germans had died in the battle, which lasted for most of the day.

The assassins were dead, but the reprisals were far from over. In fact, the fates of Gabcik and Kubis are largely overlooked in comparison to the mention of Lidice, the most notorious target of Nazi vengeance. The Gestapo and SS began a program of ruthless murder in Czechoslovakia which eventually left some 5,000 Czechs dead, and Lidice, considered a hotbed of resistance by the Nazis, would be completely destroyed. "On the day of Heydrich's state funeral [...] the village of Lidice, near Prague, was set on fire and entirely leveled by the SS for allegedly sheltering the parachute agents. Two hundred male inhabitants were shot on the spot, its female population sent to concentration camps, and the children given to German families for adoption. [...] In an act of spontaneous solidarity, several localities in the United States adopted its name." (Hauner, 2007, 88).

Pictures of massacred victims at Lidice

A picture of Lidice in the wake of the Nazis' destruction of it

Out of the children given up for adoption, only 21 of the 102 survived. The other 81 were sent to Poland, crammed into a "gas van," and asphyxiated with exhaust fumes, a method so cruel that the SS and SD themselves eventually abandoned it due to the psychological shock caused by the sounds coming from inside the vans during the gassing process. The Germans exterminated another village on the day when the parachutists died in the church crypt, in revenge for the men's escape through suicide.

One of the Nazis' gas vans

Photographs still survive showing the ground littered with the corpses with Czech men executed by the Nazis during the revenge killings that followed. Guards drove bands of Jews out of their barracks in the concentration camps and gunned them down in reprisal for what the Nazis termed "a plot by the international Jewish conspiracy." Only with the coming of autumn did the killing abate, leaving a shocked and cowed Czechoslovakia in its wake.

Chapter 7: The Significance of Heydrich's Assassination

Although the event is still well-known today, the assassination of Reinhard Heydrich failed to achieve the results desired by its architects. If anything, despite the careful planning and dramatic, spy-thriller appeal of the Czech patriots' doomed mission deep into the Third Reich, the scheme arguably caused far more harm than good.

Though Heydrich occupied a place far up in the Nazi hierarchy and exercised direct control over the extermination programs, Adolf Eichmann and others readily substituted for him in an operational sense following his demise. Though he organized the Einsatzgruppen, whose members reluctantly shot tens of thousands of people to death in the first years of the war; took a major role in the Wannsee Conference, where the fate of Europe's Jews was decided; ran the Gestapo and its dreaded "Night and Fog" program efficiently; and helped organize mass deportations and exterminations, Reinhard Heydrich proved, in the actual event, to be easily replaceable.

Eichmann

The wheels of Hitler's ghoulish extermination scheme rolled on with well-oiled efficiency in the wake of Heydrich's death. Indeed, the Nazis accelerated the pace of human extirpation towards its logical limits following the assassination, in revenge for – and in honor of – their slain colleague. The Gestapo general's killing prompted the horrors of "Operation Reinhardt," named for the Blond Beast: "During the first five weeks of the killing operation in Treblinka, between July 23 and August 28, about 245,000 Jews were deported there from the Warsaw ghetto and Warsaw district; from Radom district, 51,000; from Lublin district, 16,500, bringing the total in this period to about 312,500. [...] SS *Unterscharfuhrer* August Hingst, who served at that time in Treblinka, testified that "Dr. Eberl's ambition was to reach the highest possible numbers and exceed all the other camps. So many transports arrived that the disembarkation and gassing of the people could no longer be handled." (Arad, 1987, 87).

Just as Heydrich's death failed to impact the practical implementation of the Final Solution and other Nazi butchery, so it proved militarily insignificant. Heydrich's role was that of a secret police chief and mass murderer, and though he was recklessly brave in combat, Heydrich never commanded German armies, so his death made no military difference to the course of the war. The Third Reich's fighting machine remained the finest in the world at the time, though burdened by a factor ultimately proving to be its undoing: the incompetent, megalomaniac interference of Adolf Hitler in strategic planning.

The hope that the bold assassination would trigger greater resistance among the Czechs also backfired resoundingly on Operation Anthropoid's planners. Czechoslovakia, despite its relatively favored status in the Reich, resented the Nazi invasion, and "a non-communist resistance had existed from the beginning of the German occupation, and after almost complete destruction [...] was reorganized in 1943 and 1944." (Skilling, 1960, 181). Heydrich's death, however, prompted such a violent retaliation from the Germans that it set back the resistance's timetable rather than advancing it. The Nazi terror cowed the Czechs for several years, leaving it to the ethnic Slovaks to stage an armed rebellion against the Nazis in autumn 1944. "[T]he Slovak people [...] carried through their own liberation before the arrival of the Red Army and, for approximately two months, governed themselves through the Slovak national council. [...] In 1944, plans were laid for an uprising, and with the approval of Benes, Lieutenant-Colonel Golian was appointed military commander. [...] Open revolt spread throughout the area, partisan groups and Slovak army units taking part." (Skilling, 1960, 188).

In short, Heydrich's death triggered such unbridled violence from the Germans that the ethnic Czechs remained largely supine for the rest of the occupation, and even the Slovaks only managed to arrange an uprising after years passed. This lack of active resistance during 1942, 1943, and much of 1944 cemented Czechoslovakia's position as an industrial powerhouse producing materiel for the Nazi war effort. Only when the Third Reich tottered towards collapse, and American and Soviet boots advanced onto Czech soil in 1945, did the Czechs of Prague dare to defy their Nazi conquerors again. At this juncture, "an uprising lasting four days, in which 2,000 lives were lost, demonstrated that the Czechs were not willing passively to await their liberation." (Skilling, 1960, 195). Though it is doubtful Czechoslovakia could have mustered the strength to throw off the grip of Hitler's colossal war machine earlier than mid-1945, it is equally clear that the assassination failed to inspire significant resistance and resulted in its temporary suppression.

Having failed to alter the course of the war itself, the Final Solution (other than perhaps to hasten it), or the Czech resistance (save to weaken it through liquidation and terror), it is still fair to ask what the assassination of Reinhard Heydrich achieved. Since the Allies would certainly have hanged the Gestapo general at Nuremberg following the war if he survived that long, the bold, daring, and courageously executed plan resulted in one deeply tragic consequence: pointlessly trading the lives of some 5,000 Czechs and perhaps thousands of Jews for a single German life doomed sooner or later regardless of the plot's outcome. It is, however, possible that the man at the heart of the scheme, the exiled Czech president Eduard Benes, reaped precisely what he sought, generating hatred for the Germans and support for himself regardless of the horrible cost borne by his nation and the men and women forced to live under the Third Reich's yoke.

Intriguingly, Heydrich acted as a much more caring father than his intensely abusive parents had before him. His son Klaus died in 1943, but the other three Heydrich children survived into adulthood and lived for many decades after the World War. At least two are still alive as of 2015, and due to their relatively kind treatment by Reinhard, none of them proved fully capable of believing the horrors their father committed in the name of racial purity and the Thousand Year Reich, despite the overwhelming evidence of his guilt. "'Was my father an evil man?' Silke Heydrich asks rhetorically, recalling her relations with Reinhard Heydrich, the Nazi boss of Czechoslovakia. 'If he really was, I should be able to feel this within myself. I have watched myself for a long time and didn't feel anything of the sort.'" (Moskau, 1971, 5).

Heydrich's sons evidently received the same level of care and attention from their father as did their sisters. Heider not only absolved Heydrich himself of any wrongdoing in his mind but also could not bring himself to believe that the Third Reich itself was a criminal government on a par with Stalin's brutal, mass-murdering communist regime or the savage executioners of Mao Zedong's "Great Leap Forward:" "Heider Heydrich is an engineer at a Munich aircraft factory. 'I don't want to judge the Third Reich,' he says matter-of-factly. 'I only deal with tangible things. I want to get ahead and not be held up by the past.' Silke says her brother for a long time simply refused to believe reports about the concentration camps." (Moskau, 1971, 5).

Heydrich's wife Lina, who boasted of feeling like a "princess" while her husband ruled Czechoslovakia with an iron hand, likewise adopted a reflexive denialism after the war. Heinz Heydrich, Reinhard's younger brother, proved himself the only member of the Heydrich clan capable of facing the hard facts directly. Reinhard Tristan Heydrich, named for two tragic heroes from the pages of opera, truly acted the part of a villain throughout his life. It was Heinz, bearing a name which sounds unfortunately comical to English ears, who actually rose to achieve heroic stature and met a tragic end because of his probity. Heinz, personally revolted and horrified by the Holocaust, worked to save as many Jews and other targets of Nazi persecution as possible. He was "a journalist and the publisher of the soldiers' newspaper *Die Panzerfaust*" (Dederichs, 2009, 165), named for the Panzerfaust or "armored fist" antitank weapon, a short-range but highly-effective man-portable recoilless rocket capable of knocking out practically any Allied armored vehicle. Heinz used his newspaper's printing facilities to secretly forge false identity papers for hundreds of Jews and other political targets of Hitler's regime, enabling their escape from Nazi-occupied territory.

Unfortunately, a Nazi state attorney investigated *Die Panzerfaust* in late 1944, shortly before the fall of Nazi Germany. Heinz Heydrich believed that the Fuhrer or Himmler scented his activities and intended to close in for the kill. Fearing for his family's safety, and likely dreading prolonged torture at the hands of the Gestapo, "he shot himself in a special train fitted out with its own print-shop near the front in East Prussia." (Dederichs, 2009, 165).

Tragically, his suicide proved wholly unnecessary. The investigation centered on problems and possible corruption in the logistical branch handling distribution of paper supplies to various Nazi printing offices. Nobody in the Nazi hierarchy suspected Heinz Heydrich of his noble rescue of Jews and other potential Nazi victims. In fact, his role in this area only emerged after the end of the Second World War, when some of those he assisted came forward to testify.

Online Resources

The Capture and Trial of Adolf Eichmann: The History of Israel's Abduction and Execution of the Holocaust's Architect by Charles River Editors

The Beer Hall Putsch: The History and Legacy of Adolf Hitler and the Nazi Party's Failed Coup Attempt in 1923 by Charles River Editors

The Burning of the Reichstag: The History of the Controversial Fire That Led to the Rise of Nazi Germany by Charles River Editors

The Night of the Long Knives: The History and Legacy of Adolf Hitler's Notorious Purge of the SA by Charles River Editors

The Controversial Flight and Capture of Rudolf Hess: The History and Legacy of the Deputy Fuhrer's Mysterious Peace Mission to Britain by Charles River Editors

Bibliography

Arad, Yitzhak. *Belzec, Sobibor, Treblinka: The Operation Reinhard Death Camps.* Indianapolis, 1987.

Burian, Michal, et al. *Assassination: Operation Anthropoid, 1941-1942.* Prague, 2002. Dederichs, Mario R. *Heydrich: The Face of Evil.* Drexel Hill, 2009. (U.S. reprint.)

Defalque, Ray J., M.D. "The Puzzling Death of Reinhard Heydrich." *Bulletin of Anesthesia History.* Volume 27, Number 1 (January 29), pp. 1-7.

Gerwarth, Robert. *Hitler's Hangman: the Life of Heydrich.* New Haven, 2011.

Hauner, Milan. "Terrorism and Heroism: The Assassination of Reinhard Heydrich." *World Policy Journal.* Volume 24, Number 2 (Summer 2007), pp. 85-89.

MacDonald, Callum. *The Assassination of Reinhard Heydrich.* Edinburgh, 2007.

Moskau, Joachim. "Nazi Children Reflect on Dad." *Boca Raton News.* December 28th, 1971 issue, page 5.

Read, Anthony. *The Devil's Disciples: Hitler's Inner Circle.* New York, 2004.

Skilling, H. Gordon. "The Czechoslovak Struggle for Liberation in World War II." *The Slavonic and East European Review.* Volume 39, Number 92; Dec. 1960, pp. 174-197.

Made in the USA
Monee, IL
03 November 2023